An Early Career Book

careers in
COMPUTERS

Jo Anne Ray

photographs by
Milton J. Blumenfeld

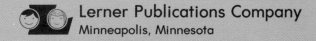

Lerner Publications Company
Minneapolis, Minnesota

LIBRARY OF CONGRESS CATALOGING IN PUBLICATION DATA

Ray, Jo Anne.
Careers in computers.

(An Early Career Book)
SUMMARY: An introduction to the varied careers in the
computer field including design engineer, programmer, keypunch operator, assembler, production foreman, and others.

1. Computers—Vocational guidance—Juvenile literature. 2.
Electronic data processing—Vocational guidance—Juvenile literature. [1. Computers—Vocational guidance. 2. Electronic
data processing—Vocational guidance] I. Blumenfeld, Milton J.,
illus. II. Title.

QA76.25.R39   001.6′023   72-7647
ISBN 0-8225-0307-7

International Standard Book Number: 0-8225-0307-7   Library of Congress Catalog Card Number: 72-7647

Second Printing 1974

Would you like to work with computers?

The computer is a machine that people use to find answers to many problems. When a computer is given certain information, it can solve a problem faster than people can.

The computer can find the answers to many problems, but it cannot think. People must do the thinking. They put the information into the computer. They also tell the computer what to do.

It takes many, many people to make and operate computers. These people must work very carefully because if they make a mistake in their jobs, the computer's answers will be wrong.

DESIGN ENGINEER

A computer looks very plain on the outside. But inside it is very *complex*—this means it is made up of many parts that must all work together. Each part of a computer is *designed*, or planned, by a design engineer. For example, one engineer plans the electrical part of a computer. He draws a plan that shows where every wire and bolt should go. Then he builds a test model. If the test model works, the company will begin making the electrical part of the computer.

The design engineer likes working with numbers. He also likes to keep working at a problem until he finds the answer.

PRODUCTION ENGINEER

The production engineer studies the design engineer's plan. He figures out a way for workers to *assemble*, or put together, the computer part. In this picture he is talking to a *mechanical engineer*—someone who knows all about machines and how they work. Together they write out step-by-step instructions for putting each computer part together. If the workers have trouble putting the part together, the production engineer finds out what is wrong.

Do you like to work with puzzles? Each part of a computer is like a puzzle to the production engineer. He must find the quickest and best way of putting it together.

PRODUCTION FOREMAN

The production foreman explains the written instructions for assembling a computer part to the workers who put the part together. He checks to see that the part is assembled correctly. He also makes sure that the workers follow a *time schedule*—a plan for putting each part together in a certain amount of time.

The production foreman likes to help people do their jobs. He always gives instructions very carefully.

ASSEMBLER

The assembler puts the computer parts together. Many computer parts are very tiny. The wire that the assembler is handling in this picture is so small that she must look at it through a microscope. An assembler must have good eyes and be able to handle tiny objects with her fingers.

The computer assembler is a very careful worker. Her job is important because the computer will not work unless all its parts are put together in the right way.

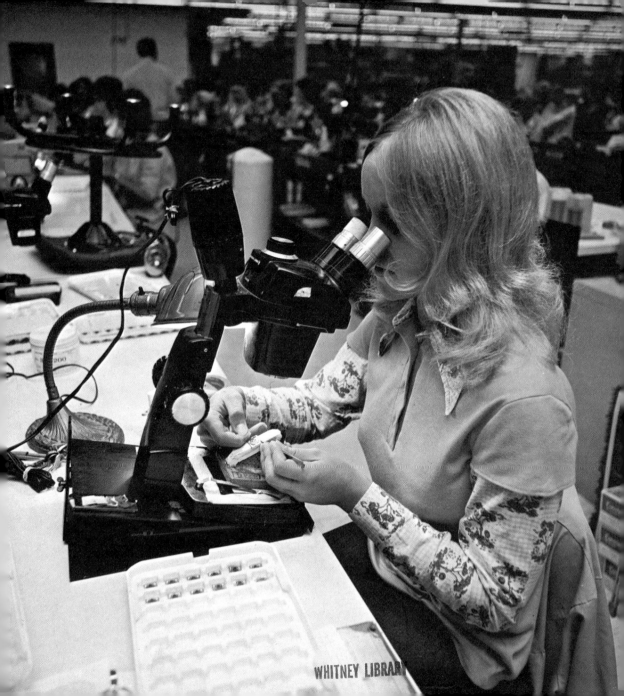

ELECTRICAL TECHNICIAN

The electrical technician tests all the electrical parts of a computer to see that they work. If something is wrong, he must find out what it is and fix it. The electrical technician knows a lot about electricity. He looks at a *blueprint*—a special kind of drawing that shows everything inside a computer part. Then he compares the blueprint with the real part to see that everything is where it should be.

The electrical technician needs very special training. He has to take machines apart and put them back together again.

QUALITY ASSURANCE TECHNICIAN

Everything that makes up a computer is tested before the computer is put together. The quality assurance technician tests the *basic materials*—the wires, metals, and plastics.

The quality assurance technician knows what each material must be like. She tests the wires, metals, and plastics with special instruments. If something is wrong with the materials, she reports it. Then different materials will have to be used.

QUALITY ASSURANCE ENGINEER

The quality assurance engineer is the last person to check the computer parts to see that they work correctly. When he says that everything is OK, the parts are put together to make a computer.

The quality assurance engineer knows how computers operate. He knows how to test every part of a computer to make sure that it will work when the computer is put together.

PACKAGING ENGINEER

Before a computer can be sent to a customer, it must be packed very carefully. The packaging engineer designs the package that holds the computer. He designs a different package for every kind of computer. There are many things a packaging engineer must know before he designs a package. He has to find out if the computer is going to be sent by truck, train, airplane, or boat. He also measures the computer to find out what size package will be needed so that the computer will not be shaken or bumped.

When the packaging engineer has all the information he needs, he knows how to pack a computer so that it will not be damaged before it reaches the customer.

TECHNICAL ILLUSTRATOR
AND TECHNICAL WRITER

A special book is packed with the computer and sent to the customer. The book uses pictures and words to tell the customer how the computer works. The technical illustrator draws the pictures for this book. He knows how to draw a special kind of picture showing what is inside a computer part. In this photograph you see him working at a big drawing board. The technical writer uses words to explain what the customer must do to make the computer work. He must choose his words very carefully so that the customer will understand his instructions.

The technical illustrator and the technical writer have difficult jobs. They must show the customer how a very complex machine works.

CUSTOMER ENGINEER

Sometimes the customer has problems with his computer that he cannot solve. Then the company that made the computer sends a customer engineer to find out what is wrong. The customer engineer uses special tools and tests to find out why the computer isn't working right. When he has found the trouble, he fixes the computer.

The customer engineer is a very good mechanic. He knows how all the computer parts work and what can go wrong with them.

SYSTEMS ANALYST

The systems analyst studies the ways a computer can help companies do their jobs. He finds out if a company can get a job done better and faster with the help of a computer. The systems analyst talks to people in a company to find out how a job is done. Then he writes a report explaining how the computer can do the same job.

The systems analyst likes to find ways for companies to save time and money by using a computer.

PROGRAMMER

A computer cannot solve a problem or do a job by itself. The programmer tells the computer what to do. He writes out a set of instructions for each job. The set of instructions is called a *program*. After he writes a program, he tests it on the computer to make sure his instructions are correct. The programmer knows what information the computer must have to do a job. He also knows how to put this information into a *code*, or special language, that the computer can use.

The programmer works very carefully. If he makes even one mistake, the computer cannot give the correct answers.

KEYPUNCH OPERATOR

The keypunch operator puts information into a code that the computer can use. She uses a machine that is like a typewriter. But instead of typing words on a sheet of paper, this machine punches holes in small cards. The punches on the cards are a code to the computer. The cards give the computer the information it needs to do a job.

The keypunch operator is like a good typist. She can punch the keys rapidly and does not make mistakes.

COMPUTER OPERATOR

The computer operator puts information into the computer. There are several different ways a computer can receive information. Sometimes the punched cards are used. Sometimes information is put into the computer on reels of tape. The operator in this picture is putting information on tape into the computer.

A computer operator knows how a computer works. He has had very special training for his job.

INSTRUCTOR

Companies that make computers have special classes where people go to learn about computers. The instructor teaches these classes. He draws a *diagram*, or picture, of a computer, showing his students its many different parts. He also explains how information is put into a code that the computer can use. When the instructor's students finish his class, they know how to be computer operators and programmers.

The instructor likes to help people learn. Someday an instructor may help you learn about computers so that you can do one of these jobs.

Computer careers described in this book

Design Engineer

Production Engineer

Production Foreman

Assembler

Electrical Technician

Quality Assurance Technician

Quality Assurance Engineer

Packaging Engineer

Technical Illustrator and Technical Writer

Customer Engineer

Systems Analyst

Programmer

Keypunch Operator

Computer Operator

Instructor

A letter from a computer industry executive

CONTROL DATA
CORPORATION

8100 34TH AVENUE SOUTH
MINNEAPOLIS, MINNESOTA

Dear Readers,

Now that you have read this book, we hope
that you know more about how computers are
made and what they do. We also hope that
you have learned about the many kinds of
jobs in the computer industry.

Soon you may be using a terminal connected
to a computer in your classroom. Many schools
are already using computers to help students
with their schoolwork.

It takes many people to make sure that computers work correctly. When you are old
enough to begin working, maybe you will want
to be one of these people.

Sincerely,

K. R. Nichols

K. R. Nichols
Control Data Corporation

The publisher would like to thank Control Data Corporation for its cooperation in the preparation of this book.

We specialize in publishing quality books for
young people. For a complete list please write

LERNER PUBLICATIONS COMPANY
241 First Avenue North, Minneapolis, Minnesota 55401